this is how you fly

a book of poetry

RACHEL TOALSON

Other Books by Rachel

Poetry
this is how you know
Life: a definition of terms
The Book of Uncommon Hours: haiku poetry
Textbook of an Ordinary Life
this is how you live
Sincerely Yours
Textbook of a Parenthetical Life
Textbook of an Extraordinary Life

Essay
Parenthood: Has Anyone Seen My Sanity?
The Life-Changing Madness of Tidying Up After Children
This Life With Boys
We Count it All Joy: Essays
Hills I'll Probably Lie Down On
If These Walls Could Talk
The Days are Long, But the Years Are Short
Life's Little Lessons: 100 Micro Essays

To see all the books Rachel has written, please click or visit the link below:
www.racheltoalson.com/writing

this is how you
fly

BATLEE
PRESS

Published by
Batlee Press
Post Office Box 591484
San Antonio, TX 78259

Copyright ©2024 by Rachel Toalson
All rights reserved.
Printed in the United States of America.
Interior design by Toalson Media.
Cover design by Ben Toalson. www.toalsonmarketing.com

No part of this book may be reproduced or transmitted in any form or by any means, electronic or mechanical, including photocopying and recording, or by any information storage and retrieval system, without permission in writing from the publisher. For information regarding permission, write to Batlee Press, PO Box 591484, San Antonio, TX 78259.

The author appreciates your taking the time to read her work. Please consider leaving a review wherever you bought it and telling your friends how much you enjoyed it. Both of those help get the book into the hands of new readers, which is incredibly important for authors. Thank you for your support.
www.racheltoalson.com

Names: Toalson, Rachel, author.
Title: This is how you fly / Rachel Toalson
Description: First edition. | Batlee Press, Texas:
Batlee Press Books, 2024

10 9 8 7 6 5 4 3 2 1

First Edition—2024

*For all my friends and family
who pulled me through a pandemic—
you know who you are*

Introduction

This book has been stuck in limbo for so long. Not because I didn't have time to work on it. I could have made the time. I didn't want to. Because I wasn't yet ready to face the pandemic again.

The poems collected here were written during the COVID-19 pandemic that, for my family and me, began in March 2020, with my kids' extended spring break that bled into summer that became their first nine weeks of a new school year. It was an inconceivably challenging time, two parents trying to monitor six kids' school work (including a kindergartener when the fall semester began) on six different devices—most of them ancient and slow—while still trying to work their full-time jobs from home, while our toilet paper supply slowly diminished (a very real anxiety for me that is only funny looking back). I had no extended time to write, so what came out of that time period was poetry. I was desperate to express myself and also process what was happening in our lives and in the world.

I wrote all during 2020; all during 2021, when we faced a new normal and still felt the (necessary) restrictions that kept us from traveling and socializing in the ways we'd done before COVID-19; and on into 2022, when we began to get out and about again. Cautiously. Hopefully.

The three parts of this book represent those three

very different times—"bound" representing the worst of COVID-19, when we sheltered in place at home and I stared at our walls with no end in sight; "but breaking" representing the slight freedoms we enjoyed as restrictions began to lift and people began masking; and "free" representing the careful freedom we observed after getting our vaccinations and learning a new normal. These three parts also, of course, represent the journey of the body and the mind.

Many suffered with mental health issues nationwide during those first years of COVID-19—and many are still suffering. I hope that these poems will strike a chord with those of us who are still processing and living in the aftermath—which is all of us—and provide a light in whatever darkness remains. May you find peace, may you find hope, and may you find joy for the days you are given.

And most of all, may you find love that will light the dark.

bound

1

How do you write
when questions swarm?

> what's for dinner
> what should they do for online learning
> where are their library books
> > that must be returned tomorrow
> why is he still getting into things
> where are all the devices
> what do I need to do today
> what will I actually get done today
> how long has it been since he showered
> how much longer will this last
> when will my head stop swimming
> who's crying now
> did I remember to put the laundry in the dryer
> what did the chicken say to the chicken
> > who crossed the road
> what begins with a T and ends with a T
> > and holds T in it
> will you tickle my back

questions inside your head
questions flying from them
so many words everywhere

but they're not the right words
all crammed up inside

and yet somehow you pick up your pen
you string words together
you write

this is how
you seize a day

2

Today you are irritated
by everything they do:
      the questions they ask,
the acts they impulsively commit,
          the cups and plates and
papers and clothes
      they leave lying around.
You feel burned out after
some hard and busy weeks
and you wonder if you'll ever
climb your way back into appreciation
for all you have.

You know you're lucky.
It's easy to forget sometimes.

And then you start reading a book
about a woman who lost
her husband and sons
in a tsunami and
she speaks about
the cups and plates and
papers and clothes you take for granted
and how much she misses them
and the gigantic chasm of emptiness

that swallows her nearly every day.

And you remember
to kiss them goodnight,
irritation curbed for the day.

This is how
you remember,
              at least for today,
that they are gifts.

3

Today he climbs in your lap,
over your lap,
through your lap,
all the way behind you,
pulls you back so you squish him,
grabs both sides of your head
so he can position it just so,
whispers loudly in your ear,
I lost one pound today and
now I weigh forty pounds.
You smile, he smiles,
he pulls you close again to whisper,
I want to play with your hair,
you let your hair down,
he brushes it in your eyes, laughs,

and even though you're trying to read,
you don't mind his whispers,
his hands tangling your hair,
his bumps and pushes—

there aren't many moments
like this anymore;
you're in quarantine and he's
with his brothers most of the time,

so you take what you can get.

You kiss his hands, his arms,
the side of his head when he leans close
to whisper one more important thing:

I love you, Mama.

This is how
you make the most of
a fleeting moment.

4

They're bickering.

They've been bickering all day.

You're tired. He's tired.
They're tired. Everyone's tired.

You say, *How about a dance party?*

Everybody groans.

You turn on the music anyway.

You shake your hips, shimmy,
do some fancier moves you learned
from Apple dance.

They giggle. Some join your exuberant,
completely over-the-top display.
Some watch, shaking their heads.
They would not join even if you paid them.

But there are smiles all around.
No one's bickering.
Everyone's forgotten they're tired.

This is how
you win a contentious afternoon.

5

today you go through the motions—
>prepare their breakfast
>clean up
>prepare their lunch
>clean up
>do some work
>break up arguments
>send them out to play
>break up more arguments
>wish you'd taken a nap
>answer four billion whys
>remind them tech time's over
>remind them again
>prepare their dinner
>clean up
>read some stories

one day is so like another
you wonder what it all means
how anyone could be happy
in such a tiny cage
why you don't just give up

you remind yourself
not every day can be a joy party

this is how
you cut yourself some slack

6

You try not to yell, shout, scream
into a pillow the frustration
that consumes your
whole body

Some days are like that
You've learned this by now
It's part of raising humans
It's part of being human

Everybody gets overwhelmed
sometimes, you tell yourself
Everybody needs a break
You are not a bad mom

This is how
you remind yourself you're enough

7

He brings you flowers,
tiny bits of paper,
mementos he finds and picks up
because he was thinking of you.
*So you'll remember
I love you*, he says.

These are everyday offerings.

Tonight he reads you
a story about elephants.
Male elephants leave the group
to live with other elephants.
He stops. *I would never do that*, he says.
I would stay with my mama.

You smile.
*Your mama would let you
stay with her as long as
you wanted*, you say.

Forever, he says.

Forever, you say.

You move on
to a quick workout.
He interrupts you for a kiss.

You're delightful, you say.

He runs away.
You watch him until
he disappears.
You know he'll be back.

This is how
you enjoy your last son.

8

    You wonder:
*Is this the way it will be
from now until eternity?*
    You wonder:
*How will I ever
get anything done?*
    You wonder:
*What if I took
the pressure off?*

    You wonder
what it might be like
to join their relay races
out in the cul-de-sac.
    You wonder
why you didn't do this
a long time ago.

This is how
you make the most of
your circumstances.

9

fresh bread cools in the pan
it's been ages since you made it
the aroma reaches into
the corner of every room
        stretches
        swirls
        settles on the six of them
waiting without words
for the first warm buttery slice

this is how
you remember the smell
of easier days

10

Their noises grate

It's been too long
cooped up like this, you think
You still have the whole
summer to go, you think
You're so tired, you think

The thoughts could
carry you away to a darker,
lower, more frightening place
so you gather them up,
sweep them into a tidy dust pile,
and release them to the wind

Let's go for a jog, you say

They complain, argue,
moan that they can't find their shoes

Before you begin,
you tell them, *One gratitude mile*
Think of all the things
you're thankful for
while we run

Halfway back home
you call out some of your thankfuls
Halfway back home
they start doing the same

The sun!
Wide open space!
Green grass!
Toys to play with during quarantine!
Books!
Puzzles!
A big backyard!
Parents who love us!
Kids who love their parents!

This is how
you turn a doomed day
around

11

He called today and said
he wanted to go home.
It was a rough weekend,
            he's tired,
he hasn't been able to
keep up with his school work,
      he needs a break,
the commas under his eyes
have become more pronounced,
he hasn't been sleeping well
on top of all that,

           can you please
           just take him home?

You study his face for a moment,
the sharpening angles
and the pleading eyes.
You wish you could let him go home,
but you know that running away
never solved anything.
So you say, *I'm sorry, buddy.*
We'll have to find another solution.

And he doesn't fight.

Maybe he's done fighting.
Maybe that scares you.

You tell him the two of you
will talk at home.
He finishes the day,
rides the bus home,
sits on the couch,
waits for the plan
for how to get him caught up.
You make one together.
He puts it on the refrigerator,
a reminder of what you're both
committed to do.

This is how
you take it one day at a time.

12

Today the noise at the table
is a little above what
you can normally handle
> (your Apple Watch confirms
> it's outside the healthy range
> for your ears)

three conversations happening
at the same time.

Your twelve-year-old
turns to you and says,
*I love how chaotic and yet
manageable our family is.*

You think, if only he knew
> how close you are to breaking
> how not-manageable it feels on a daily basis
> how often you long for silence

But you smile
at him anyway.

This is how
you manage an
unmanageable moment.

13

You made the effort
booked the time
gathered the necessary safety requirements

but the problem is
you can't always prepare
for everything that might trip you up

and this time it was a tiny little lip
a concerted effort
a moment of attention lag

and you flew too fast to react
just skidded to a stop
it knocked the breath out of you

but you climbed back to your feet
dusted off an aching knee
and kept on running home

This is how
you conquer the unexpected

14

It always catches you unaware,
the altercation that will
make it hard to sleep.
This one comes only five minutes
before you're supposed to go to bed.

You hear them scuffling
in the doorway of your bedroom—
he doesn't think he should
have to surrender his phone,
his father has already taken it
for the evening.
He lunges, tries to grab it
out of his father's hands,
but he's smaller, lighter—
at least for now.
He loses the battle,
but does he, really?

You lie in bed,
tossing and turning,
a question haunting you:

        Is he safe with himself?

You say it out loud.

I think so, his father says.

You check anyway.

He sits putting Legos together,
scarcely looks up when you
poke your head inside his room.

You ask him the question:
>*Are you safe with yourself?*

Yeah, he says.

You watch him a moment longer.
Just leave your door open, okay?

He doesn't answer.
Maybe he didn't hear you.

He leaves the door open.

You check on him three more times,
then finally go to bed.

This is how
you try to reassure yourself

of what cannot be assured.

15

Today you feel the spinning of your mind
        so much to think about
    so much to do
you're not sure you can handle it all
but they're depending on you—

    what's the writing prompt
    what do I do for math
    how do I finish this science
    do you remember history
    can I take an AR test

You think about taking
the next several weeks off work
you can't concentrate anyway
but you're not sure when this will end
        if it will ever end
and you need that time
you need to write

despite it all—
    the inability to concentrate
    the constant overwhelming pressure
    the incessant interruptions—
you need to write

So you close your door
        take a deep breath
                and put pen to paper

This is how
you show the coronavirus
who's boss

16

Sometimes you think
you've reached the end of your rope
and there's nothing left to do
but keep

        walking
        crawling
        sliding face first

Somehow you go on

This is how
you endure

17

Some days you handle it
better than others.

Yesterday, for example,
they laughed and shouted and argued
and whined and bounced off the walls
all day, and you had patience enough
to repeat your *Please lower your voices* and
Please take your rowdiness outside and
*Please go spend some time in
separate places so you're not
tempted to argue.*

Today, though, you have
ten minutes of it and are done.
You must have woken up
on the wrong side of…
whatever.
Or maybe you're just tired.
Or burned out.
Or…

You should probably
be kinder to yourself.

So you shut your bedroom door,
stretch out on your bed,
and take a nap.

This is how
you reset.

18

This is where he flies into a rage
      destroying things
           screaming
                threatening
           terrorizing
    leaving a burning path of
I don't feel safe here

This is where you think
        We're not going to make it
        here's the end of things
        watch it all crumble

This is where you cry

This is where you rub away
the heartache while you
try not to think about
    what's next
    how much will he destroy
    when will this end

This is where you wonder
                Why me

This is where the world flips
empties out
spiders into cracks
too large to mend

This is where you
close your eyes and breathe
>   one
>   two
>   three
>   four hundred seventy-nine

This is where you say
Not today
Not here
Not him

This is where you
hold fast to love

This is where
you forgive

This is where
you find a way to say
I believe you are good
>   *my precious son*

This is how
you beat back the demons
with a spike-studded sword

19

Want to go on a date?
He grins.

You haven't been on a date
in more than six months,
since an extended Spring Break
heralded the beginning
of a new pandemic reality.

Yes, you say.
It doesn't even matter where you go.
You haven't sat anywhere without kids
in seven months.

It's the first day
your kids are back in school—
October already—and as soon as
they're tucked away in classes,
you meet in the car,
drive to your favorite restaurant,
share a plate of Tex-Mex enchiladas,
laugh over margaritas,
eat way too many chips.
You walk it off to Barnes & Noble,
browse a little, like you don't remember

there's a highly contagious illness out there
(except for the mask that folds off
your peripheral vision and makes it easy
to trip over curbs),
and finish the date with frozen yogurt.
Mostly like the old days,
if not exactly.

You return home so full
you wonder if you'll eat dinner
(but of course hunger returns).

Just inside the door
you embrace.

This is how
you remember life goes on.

20

You listen to them panic

> *Where's my ID*
> *I can't find my lunch box*
> *I put my water bottle right here and now it's gone*

You feel bad for not stepping in.
You tell yourself you should step in.
You change your mind.
They moan and complain about their luck.
You saw the lunch box
on the counter this morning,
you can see the missing water bottle
from where you stand,
you have no idea where the ID is.

You point and direct;
they don't look very well.

When the house is empty you say,
They're old enough to do this on their own.

Agreed, their father says.
We should charge for our services.

You weren't going to go that far,
but then again—it's not a bad idea.

They're growing up.

This is how
you grow them up.

21

This morning your son
draws a turkey comic
on a sheet of paper,
writes the words, *I'm thankful for*,
leaves blanks for his brothers to fill in.
You watch him make five copies,
watch him set them in the proper places,
    along with a sharpened pencil,
watch him smile at you staring.

What? he says.

I'm thankful for you, you say.

He echoes the words,
then goes to wake his brothers.

You'll eat the feast at lunch time,
but that won't be your
favorite part of this day,
even with its eight pies,
its pumpkin cheesecake,
its macaroni and cheese and
mashed potatoes and
vegan turkey and gravy and

stuffing and salad and cranberry sauce.

This will.

Yes, you'll think.

*This is how
you make a holiday.*

22

You put the last dish on the table,
eye the feast they've been
checking on every other minute.
It took days to prepare,
and it's gone in an hour, probably less,
considering the hunger
with which they eye the spread.

For a moment you wonder
if all that effort was worth it.

And then you sit down together.
The second-oldest offers to pray.
You talk about past thanksgivings,
the people who gathered,
the people you miss this year
because of a pandemic.

Of course the effort was worth it.
You see it in their smiles,
hear it in their voices,
feel it in the warmth that robes the table,
smell it in the herbs that sprinkle the food,
taste it in your first delicious bite.

This is how
you celebrate Thanksgiving
in the middle of a pandemic.

23

Today you spend
all day fasting

working on projects
to distract you

joining friends in a sort of vigil
hoping the world doesn't elect to spend
another four years unraveling
under a madman

This is how
you pray

24

December first, he says.
Already?

You're sitting
together at the table,
kids at school,
house quiet.
It's the eighteenth anniversary
of the day he asked you
to marry him.
You're sharing a meal to celebrate,
because it's 2020,
there's a pandemic,
and every opportunity to celebrate
is one you'll take.

I know, you say.
*Seems like the days just go
faster and faster as
the years pass.*

You share a dish of
    hummus,
    pita chips,
    vegetables,

try to make the minutes
                stretch,
                elongate,
                slow down a little.

They rush like all the rest,
but you wring their joy,
wrestle out their hope,
wrap their love around you.

This is how
you end a special day.

25

You pat out pizza dough,
spread the sauce,
line up the pepperonis
and grate the cheese.
They're all wondering aloud
when dinner will be ready,
but there's no real rush;
they'll likely be up until midnight,
fireworks booming outside their window,
lighting up the frame.
He puts on a movie,
the story of a fairy tale villain,
your favorite kind,
and you all settle in to watch,
story weaving around you like
the cold that sneaks in through the door
when one of them lets in the cat.

You find an early countdown,
pour some sparkling water,
cheer the new year,
then send them off to bed
so you can eat your Olive Garden
in peace.

This is how
you ring in a new year.

26

You pull out new games
from the closet.
We'll play all these today? they say.

Yep.

Together?

Yep.

They've been asking
for a family game night for weeks.
Today you give them
a whole family game day.

You strategize, you play, you
laugh laugh laugh.

This is how
you welcome a new year.

27

You get up early, even though
you didn't get much sleep,
because today's a scheduled long run
and it's your only opportunity to do it.
You decide, after a shower,
to forgo workout clothes—
you'll rest for the day, unlike other days—
and pull on your softest sweatpants,
a favorite T-shirt, and
a warm sweater pullover.
It says comfortable,
with no expectation
for more movement.
You could recline on the couch all day
and read if you wanted.
(You won't,
    can't, really,
because you're a parent.)

You watch him at the table,
flipping a Rubik's cube,
another stretched out on the floor
coloring beasts with gel pens,
someone else bent over a puzzle,
one side of his lip turned up

in concentration.
You listen to the others
collaborate on a game
in the playroom, arguments left behind
for a sliver of time.

Their father sits on the end of the couch,
writing in a journal.
Every now and then
you sneak a peek.

You soak in the long legs,
the bright eyes, the hair
that curls over their ears and brows,
and you think you may know what bliss is,
at least for a few moments.

This is how
you make the most of
a day off.

28

It's the first week of the new year.

Remember this time last year,
when you made all those plans
for the months ahead?
Remember how they collapsed
almost before they had a chance to begin?

*I'm only planning for
the first quarter*, you tell him.

Makes sense, he says.

Because, you know.

Yeah, he says.

You look at each other.

*You never know when
another pandemic will
come out of nowhere*, you say
at the exact same time.

You never know.

You both laugh.

And that's it—at least,
after nine months of quarantine,
nine months of social distancing
from the friends and family you love,
nine months of the strangest times
you've ever experienced,
you are still laughing.

This is how
you approach a new year now.

29

You choke up
when remembering a year ago—
the hopes and dreams and plans you had
that didn't turn out quite like you thought.

Today you scroll through those memories,
let them eat you alive,
let them whisper,
You should have known
it would never happen.

Today you send a note
to your friend,
soaking it in maybe
a little too much emotion,
because sometimes you just
need to be reminded of
who you are and
why you're here.

And when the reply comes
across the hundred miles
you smile to yourself and think,
I have the best friends.

This is how
you remember
you're not alone.

30

Today you stop work early
even though it's not usually your style
to watch the inauguration
of the 46th president
listen to him talk about
>unity
>in a country that has sown division
>(at least the last four years)

watch him roll back injustice
with the sweep of a pen

You marvel at how beautiful
a country can be
when every man woman child
every race caste religion sexual orientation

>>person

is valued for who they are
Today a great weight
lifts from your shoulders
because you know
>you know!

hate will not win
dark will not ever squash the light

good eventually prevails

and you think
now we will make America
      compassionate
      just
      loving
again

This is how
you cry   conquer
      carry on
remembering who you are

31

You pour the batter
watch it bake
ice the layers
press peppermint pieces
into the sides and top

You knead the dough
add the butter
sprinkle the brown sugar and cinnamon
roll it up
let it rise

You scrape the chocolate
bake it just enough for
crunchy edges, gooey middle
spread white chocolate chips on top
shake out more peppermint pieces

        cake
        cinnamon rolls
        peppermint chocolate brownies:

This is how
you celebrate your baby's birthday

32

Today you watch him
sit in a big boy seat,
observe him choose his own Lego set
and an animal to adopt out in the wild,
see his face light up at
an endless succession of treats
in celebration of his birthday.

Today you ask him if he will
hold your hand on the way up the stairs,
and he agrees, for now.

Today you tuck him under
a blanket you made his brother,
kiss him goodnight,
and watch him sleep for probably
longer than you should,
with so much work to do.

Today you wonder
where the time has gone,
these six years that have
passed in a blink,
to shape him into such
a remarkable child.

Today he breaks your heart
with his growing
and yet deepens your joy
with his brilliance.

This is how
you marvel at life's paradoxes.

33

You made your own cake
for your birthday.

That's sad, one of your sons says.
*But it's probably better than
the one we would have made you.*

You wonder if anyone
will remember it's your birthday
when you drag yourself from bed
for your morning run,
long before anyone else is up.

But you hear them whispering
outside your room after you shower.
And when you walk into the kitchen,
there's the cake you made,
candles covering it.
All of them grin and sing.
You try not to let your misty eyes
blind you to the moment.

Then you have cake for breakfast—
who cares if you
made it yourself?

This is how
you enjoy another birthday.

34

*Don't plan on doing
any work today*, he says.

You feel the guilt bloom
in a tiny shadow, the way
it always does when you lose
an hour or two, sometimes a whole day.
How will you ever get everything done
if you take a day off?

It's your birthday, he says,
like he can read your mind.

Even on your birthday
you find it difficult to excuse yourself
from the work you love.
But you do.

And he takes you to a movie and dinner
and you walk around Target holding hands
and sit in the car holding hands and
you talk and talk and talk and
you don't stay out too late because
your routines are more solid than liquid,
and, besides, you've been out all day,

you don't want too much of a good thing,

and on the drive home you remember
he's the one who still holds your heart
even after all these years
and you're glad you took a day off
to spend some time alone with him
because

this is how
you reconnect.

35

You drive to the familiar meeting place,
beating your mom for the first time

You're so excited to drop them off
because it's your birthday weekend
and it's been such a long time
since you could breathe,
just the two of you

You kiss them all,
wave them gone

He turns to you and says,
What do you want to do?
and you say *I don't know,
what do you want to do?*
and he says *I don't know,
what do you want to do?*
and you say, *I don't know,
what do you want to do?*
and he says, *I don't know,*
he looks at you sideways,
what do you want to do?

You laugh at the whole world of freedom

open before you and say,
Let's eat and watch one of our shows
The same thing you do
every Friday night,
except this time no kids
to barge in the door and
interrupt

This is how
you enjoy a kidless weekend

36

Forget the numbers,
focus on the possibilities
still open to you.

Forget the aches,
remember what your body
has done for you.

Don't go looking for
new wrinkles and gray hairs,
just notice the skin still flush with life.

This is how
you age with grace.

37

Today you race through the miles—
one, two, three.
You feel good—
this body's certainly
younger than forty,
or at least it feels like it—
you don't know what you're thinking,
what steals your concentration,
where the hazard comes from
but in a second you're airborne,
headed for asphalt and—
what's that?
Some kind of utility contraption—
in a split-second you twist,   turn,
shift a little to the right,
avoid the sharp edges of metal
but forget about the pavement
that punches your
              eye
              cheek
              upper lip
              somewhere on the chin—
you pop up, shake it off.

A little skin off your face

is a worthwhile tradeoff for life,
you tell yourself—

You were never one to quit,
no matter how hard
the ground hit.

You run the remaining
three miles home,
road rash scorching you
all the way to Fire Cracker.

This is how
you prove
ain't nothing gonna keep you down.

38

You don't have power
They don't have water
You invite them over
to fill up buckets,
rinse milk gallons,
whatever thermoses they have

They invite you over
for hot tea, a little warmth
before returning to your freezing house,
some hot soup that will warm you
all the way to the deepest places

You know you won't freeze,
having friends like them

They know they won't die of thirst,
having friends like you

This is how
you survive
a winter storm in Texas

39

You sit down in your wing chair to write,
like you always do in the early morning hours,
and you hear it:
>	a thump,
>	a clatter,
>   the noises that tell you
you're not the only one awake.
You feel the annoyance gather around
your eyes and mouth,
your face likely a clear picture of it,
to be read by the early riser.

But he bursts into your room
with a sleepy smile and says,
Is it time to wake up?
and you gather him in your arms
and kiss the top of his head and
write with him on your lap.
Your handwriting's messy and
you might not even be able to read this later,
but his weight in your arms
is an unexpected gift.
He rarely does this anymore,
and you miss the weight of him
in your arms.

This is how
you embrace more unexpected
days off from school.

but breaking

40

Today you pull up a
collapsible chair in the driveway,
angle it six feet from friends,
and talk about life,
kid struggles, work woes,
all the things weighing
your heart and mind.
You used to call yourselves
Quarantine Club, because
you were trying to survive a pandemic.
Then a winter storm
slammed the state and
you shared your water,
they shared their electricity.
You made it through together.
Now you call yourselves
Survival Club.

You bike home after the gathering,
feeling stronger with
people behind you.
A team.
Friends who have become
family.

This is how
you embrace community.

41

There is a moment you realize
you are capable of leaving
your youngest child at home
and not even realizing it until
forty-five minutes down the road
and one of your sons asks
where his brother is and
you slam on the brakes
in the middle of the highway,
phone a neighbor who lets herself into
your thankfully unlocked back door
and reports to you that your son
is still home and safe—upset but safe—

and you turn around and
head immediately home to assure him
you will never leave him again
and he will say but you might
if he comes back into the house
for a bookmark like he did today,
and you will crush him in your arms
and hold him close to you and
rock and cry and kiss his face,
the relief swiftly trading places
with guilt and shame—

>how could you do this
>>how could you do this
>>>how could you do this?—

and you wonder if you're
a terrible horrible parent
for leaving a child behind
and you don't want it to happen again, ever,
so what is the contributing factor,
you analyze the morning,
the rushing to get in the car,
the hurry hurry hurry,
the immediate launching of
a scheduling meeting,

and the realization steals over you—
this life is too busy,
there's too much stress,
something needs to change.

And it's almost an instinct:
the next time
someone asks you
to do something,
you say
no.

This is how

you give yourself permission
to slow down.

42

Today you meet with
a writer friend, discuss a story
you're working on, iron out details,
make the skeleton of a plan,
agree on what next to write.
Today you laugh, brainstorm,
discuss, plan, dream, agree,
appreciate.

Today you say,
I'm really excited about this.

It's been a long time
since you could say that about
anything.

Today you think, *A friend.*
Who knew all you needed was
      a friend,
      a collaboration,
      a project
to connect you back
to yourself.

This is how

you find
your passion again.

43

When your partner says
I'm going to take the kids
to Dad's cabin for a weekend
so you can have some time to yourself

you don't say
You don't have to do that
But what about all the stuff that needs to be done?
Are you sure you want to?

You just say
That would be wonderful
and you let them go
> without question
> without guilt
> without regret.

This is how
you let yourself rest.

44

They leave,
gone for a whole weekend,

and it's strange, you think,
how quiet the house is
without all of them here,
how completely still it is,
how utterly lifeless and stagnant.

The absolute silence does not
call to you as you imagined it would;
you find words difficult to grasp,
relaxation nearly impossible,
sleep slippery once the sun sets
and the new moon peeks bashfully
into the too-dark, restless night.

It's good to be alone, you think—
necessary, even.

It's good, too,
to welcome them back.

This is how
you miss them.

45

Today you pour in one cup of flour,
he pours in the other.
You measure half a cup of sugar,
he dumps it in the mix.
You explain what a pinch of salt is,
melt the butter to pour,
watch him stir with his small hands
like a pro.

He peers into the oven,
six tartlets lined up on baking sheets.

When will they be done? he says.

What does the timer say? you say.

He counts down,
opens the oven,
sniffs the finished product
as you pull it free.

One more thing, you say
as he prepares to fling off the apron
and dash outside to report
his success to his brothers.

A little powdered sugar,
sprinkled on top.

Done? he says.

Done, you say.

You watch him leave the kitchen
licking the white dust
from his fingers.

This is how
you remember moments are
the real treasures of life
(and lemon tartlets, too).

46

*I just don't understand why you
aren't more excited about this*, he says.

All weekend you've had a grand time,
kids visiting grandparents,
the two of you enjoying dates
you don't usually get
when they're home,
since babysitting fees don't
fit in your budget.

Now you feel a rotten ending
to a lovely respite.

You shrug. *I just don't enjoy it.*
You're not unusual.
You've had this conversation
with other writers, who feel
the same way you do.
But he's completely different—
extrovert where you're introvert,
musician where you're writer,
creating for the recognition
and results it brings
where you create just for

the sheer pleasure of it.

He says other things,
things that make your heart wobble,
things he'll apologize for later,
things that make you wonder,
in your quiet way,
if there really *is* something
wrong with you.

Then you'll pack up in the car
and drive a silent ninety miles
to pick up your kids,
hoping the air will clear
once they're back home.

This is how
you sour a last day
of a kidless weekend.

47

We're different people, you know, you say.
*The things that excite you
don't necessarily excite me.*

I know, he says.
*I shouldn't have said
those things.*

He kisses your forehead,
says, *I just want you
to be successful. Happy.*

*You have to let me
figure that out*, you say.

He nods.

You join each other
in the kitchen,
warming leftovers for the kids,
memories of your weekend dates
overtaking the memory of this
last day and its semi-disaster.

You let them.

This is how
you redeem a last day of a
kidless weekend.

48

You pedal over cracked-up asphalt,
up hills,
down hills,
around corners cloaked in
cactus and prickly pear.
He points out the plants,
you nod,
he makes observations,
you nod,
he asks questions,
you answer the ones you can.
The sun smiles down on both of you,
and after you've wrestled the bikes
back into your van he says,
Can we climb that mountain?
and you think about
the order you need to
pick up from Target,
it will be rush hour soon.
You eye the mountain,
recognize its appeal,
and say, *Yes*.

You climb the mountain together
and pause to see

the world below.

This is how
you spend an afternoon date
with your son.

49

During a rare moment to yourself
you will consider all that
needs to be done—
bills to pay
piling dishes
T-shirt orders for your kids
a budget that hasn't been balanced
in too long
the quarter's taxes
emails to send
phone calls to make

But during a rare moment to yourself
you will remember how long it's been
since you sat and stared in silence
and this you will do until
the thoughts in your head quiet
and the world brightens perceptibly
and the book beside you practically speaks

You're sure it says
It's time you read me now

So you do

This is how
you re-center

50

You grin and bear it

You're not sure you should
but you do it anyway
you listen to them talk about things
that don't interest you
things they know almost nothing about
(but pretend to know everything about)
things that have nothing to do with
where this day is going

They're probably just trying
to get a rise out of you
well you refuse to rise
you plaster on your smile
or you slide from the room
you tell yourself it's not cowardly
it's self-preservation
you tell yourself if it was
something high stakes
you would stand up and argue
but the truth is you're not sure
the truth is you're tired
the truth is you've been worn down
maybe you don't care about

anything anymore
least of all setting the record straight
and sometimes…well
sometimes you just have to
walk away

The truth is you're doing
the best you can
And on your best days
you remember they are, too

You remind yourself to love your people
You remind yourself to love yourself

This is how
you survive the aftermath

51

Today he climbs in bed with you
because his brothers are
watching a movie,
in the middle of a summer
Avengers movie marathon.

You're reading. He's talking.

You put down your book,
a little surprised you don't feel
a bit of annoyance for the interruption.
He's looking at you,
talking about a book,
asking you a question,
grinning.

You grin back.

His eyes shine into yours,
and a memory reaches across the years—
those first days together,
when he was small enough
to fit in the crook of your elbow,
when you fed him by the
warm light of a lamp,

when he gazed at everything
with those large, curious eyes.

He yawns and takes your hand.
He goes back to his book,
you go back to yours,
your hands intertwined,
fingers threaded.

Today you will read one-handed,
every few minutes glancing at him,
and you will let him fall asleep
and his daddy will carry him to bed,
a little sweat spot marking the pillow,
the impression his body made remaining
even after he's gone.

This is how
you treasure today.

52

You were supposed to go
somewhere fun today.

Two of them are sick.
One of them is not sick.

The one who is not sick
whines and complains.

He wants to go
somewhere fun today.

You'd like to remind him
he was sick days ago,

and he didn't want to
go anywhere, either.

You explain
(with oh-so-much-patience)

that he is not the only person
in the world, unfortunately.

He sulks outside,

you care for the two sick,

but soon enough you all stretch out
on couches and watch a movie together.

You can't go somewhere fun today,
but at least you can do something fun at home.

Remember quarantine?
You got really good at it.

The one who whined and complained
isn't whining and complaining anymore.

The fun day ends up
a fun day.

This is how
you manage an unexpected sick day.

53

You take a test
It says you have COVID

You're angry—
               so angry—

You managed to avoid it
for almost two years

For almost two years
you have stayed home

For almost two years
you have worn a mask

For almost two years
you have socially distanced

when staying home
wasn't feasible

and then you hopped
a plane

You blame cabin fever

but really it was a false sense of security

You were vaccinated
operating on faulty information

You wore a mask
even though you were vaccinated

but you saw so many who
weren't wearing one

Who knows if they were
vaccinated or not

One of them gave you
COVID

and now you're angry—
        so angry—

and sick and tired and miserable
and worried about long-term effects

no one really knows
much about

But then your six-year-old

tests positive

and you're no longer completely
alone in your room, brooding on it all

He's there snuggling with you
dining with you, laughing with you

saying, *I'm so glad
I have COVID with you*

what a thing to say
you're not glad you got COVID

you're still
angry

but if you had to isolate with anyone
you'd pick him

You stretch out under the covers
and fall asleep

with his warm feet
pressed to your back

This is how

you find the silver lining in
I have COVID

54

Do you want to play
Clue *with me?* he says.

There are a billion things to do,
but he never asks.
He's getting older,
teenage years unfolding,
voice dropping lower,
legs and arms thickening into a man.

He wants to play *Clue?*
With you?

Let's make a date, you say.
We'll play at three o'clock.

He agrees.

The bookmarked time announces itself
with a *Ready to play now?*
He has the board out,
pieces all set up,
    killer
    weapon
    room where the crime happened

tucked away in its envelope.
He looks at you with
the same eyes he had
as a two-year-old.

You still have
so much to do.

Yes, you say.

This is how
you love your thirteen-year-old today.

55

They huddle around the table,
fitting pieces to a puzzle.
You watch their heads,
bent nearly to touching.
Their chatter's amiable,
a peal of laughter occasionally
lifting from the fold.
Their smiles, after a shared joke
that was more silly than humorous,
skip across your chest.
For a moment you think about
joining them, but you hesitate.
You don't want to break the spell.
So instead you watch.

This is how
you stop time for the barest moment.

56

You always dread this: the scale.

You have a scale at home.
You weigh yourself every day,
watch the fluctuations to make sure
they don't deviate too much.
But there's something different
about the doctor's scale—
maybe it's more official,
maybe it means something more,
maybe it will show
you've missed something.

Have you missed something?

So you wait,
one leg tapping out a beat,
one eye focused on the book
you're trying to read,
the other concentrating
on the peripheral door.

They'll call you back,
and it's the first thing they'll do:
ask you to step on the scale.

Fifteen minutes pass.
Now you just want to
get it over with.

They call you back.

You try not to look.
It doesn't matter.
It's measured in kilograms,
so the number slips right
from your head.

When you get home,
your husband asks how it went,
were there any problems,
what did the scale show—

>he knows you were
>worried about it.

To this last one, you can honestly answer,
I don't know.

It feels like a victory.

The number will be on record,
but that doesn't mean
you have to look.

This is how
you survive an encounter
with the doctor's scale.

57

You spend a whole day in town,
soaking up the sunshine,
absorbing their laughter,
watching them climb imaginary towers
and play endless games of ping pong
and challenge each other to a duel.
You cleared your schedule,
left your notebook at home,
have nothing else to do
but watch them play,
admire their skill,
keep a mental tally of all the ways
you love them so.

It's been a hard year.
You needed this.

Later you all walk to a chocolate shop
and even though they all get ice creams
and you only have enough
remaining calories in the day's count
for a small bon bon,
you relish, still,
the perfection of this day.
On the leisurely walk back to the car,

you think, *Yes*.

This is how
you remember life really is
beautiful.

58

Today you rise early for a run,
finish up a few housekeeping things,
drive to a halfway point to
pick up kids who spent a week
of their summer with grandparents.
You know the detox
will be a challenge.
You know it'll take at least
a week of effort trying to get them
back into the summer schedule.
You have a little bit of a headache
just thinking about it.

But when you see their faces,
your love balloons.
Absence makes the heart
grow fonder, after all.
You hug and
kiss them and
hug them again.

This is how
you welcome them home.

59

It's been a long time since
you sat in a car with just him.
You're not really sure what to talk about.
You let him lead.
He talks about the thing
he's building in Minecraft—
he's growing up, it's true,
but this sends you back into
the days when he was little.
Where did the time go? you think.
I don't have to say a thing, you think.
I will just listen.

He talks the entire
five miles to his job.

And it may not fix everything
between you, but at least it
offers a rickety bridge.

This is how
you love a teenager.

60

Today you may not have accomplished
everything you wanted to do,
but you loaded the dishes,
wrote a poem,
spoke mostly kindly to your kids,
kissed your partner,
got out of bed in the first place.

And sometimes that's about
all you can ask.
So rather than focus on
all you didn't do,
try celebrating all you did.

This is how
you claim victory over
a disappointing day.

61

Today you join them fitting
puzzle pieces to a Toy Story scene
Watch with them a movie adapted
from a book you recently finished together
(*They changed so many things*,
they say when it's over)
Call your mother

This is how
a lazy Saturday becomes
a day of connection

62

You weren't prepared
for the leaving-time to come so soon—
maybe you would have enjoyed
your one-on-one moments a little more,
instead of filling the wedges
with more activity,
finding tasks to check off a list,
worrying about the future.

Maybe you would have canceled everything,
just for a moment more with him.
Maybe you would have
      taken more naps,
      colored more,
      counted cars,
      baked with him,
      hugged him,
      kissed him,
      taken him all the places
           you once could have gone,
just the two of you.

But today you
spread out on the floor,
like you used to do,

set a timer for fifteen minutes
and open your gel pens.

Pink kindness? you say.

Yeah, he says.

You watch the way
his head bends over the book,
hand oh-so-careful,
pink spilling across pages.

This is how
you make the most
of your circumstances.

63

Today you hand them chalkboards
snap pictures
hug them at the doors of their schools
Their eyes shine with excitement
Yours probably do, too
A quiet house calls
It's been so long since you wrote in a quiet house

But it's bittersweet too
You know that one day there will be a last first day
You try not to think of that right now
You try to stay in the moment

You watch them disappear through doors that will
    challenge them
    mold them
    grow them a little more

You try not to think what can happen—
what has happened before, too close to home
They will be okay, you tell yourself
They have to be
It's the only possibility you can bear

This is how

you send your children
to their first day of
another school year

64

You listen to him sing downstairs,
without an audience,
simply for the joy of it,
and the rumbling sound of it,
the way he soars to the high falsetto,
makes you smile.
And you think,
I should sing more for myself, too.

This is how
you remember the
magic of music.

65

You want to go to sleep.

You want to go to sleep,
but he's in bed next to you.
The youngest child,
who will not want to
fall asleep next to you
for long.

He wants to hold your hand.

It's hard to fall asleep
when he wants to hold your hand.
He's fidgety and wiggly.

He wants to press his head
up against yours.

It's hard to fall asleep
when he presses his head
up against yours.
His hair blows in your face,
tickles your nose.

But you let him stay anyway.

You let him squeeze your fingers
like he will never let them go,
you let him try to mold your minds together.
You don't fall asleep.
You smell his forehead instead.

You know it won't last forever.
Nothing ever does.

This is how
you make the most of the
time that remains.

66

How is it already
November first? you say.

Every start of the month
feels the same—
> where did the time go?
> how do the days pass so quickly?
> when will it slow down?

You feel surprised
by every first of every month
when they ask about
> allowance
> the changing of chores
> the cleaning zone rotation.

You still haven't discovered
the secret of
slowing time.

But every first of the month
reminds you:
> Stop
> breathe

take joy in each remarkable moment.
Live this day to its fullest,

however you can.

As the days pass you'll slowly
forget that conviction,
the commitment you'd like to make
three hundred sixty-five days a year.

But another first
comes back around
to remind you:

This is how
you embrace the rhythms of a year.

67

You spend the day in town
watching them
            climb
    slide
            swing
    giggle
fumble through chess
at some community tables.
You watch them inhale their lunch
ask for more
race off to play when
they realize they've eaten
everything you packed.
You watch the way
their eyes light up when you
walk them to the fudge shop
and they see it has ice cream.

Not once do you get lost in your phone
and by the end of the day
you realize you much prefer
this kind of living.
So you make it official:
No more distractions on fun days
with your kids.

This is how
you take life by both hands
and really live.

68

You sit with friends
you haven't seen in a while.

You almost didn't come
but decided to at the last minute,
and it surprises you how much
the talk fills you up,
how being with these people,
sharing some of a heart's burdens,
makes you feel lighter,
like you might be able to handle
whatever comes next.

Sometimes you forget
how much stronger we are
together.

You sit and talk and
laugh and breathe.

You leave late,
which means you stay up too late,
which means you'll probably
have a headache tomorrow,
but what does that matter

in light of today?

Today you have everything
you need.

This is how
you remember the
power of community.

69

The smell of pine
tells you the way

you follow them all
into a white tent
all of you masked and
watching out for others

you go in search
of the perfect tree

that one's too tall
this one's not tall enough
another's out of your budget
you make the rounds again

they point
you examine
he comments
you all move on until

the perfect tree
practically trips one of them

you laugh, say,

I guess that one wants
to come home with us

everyone agrees

it lends light to your home
a little bit of hope
wrapped around
pine and bark

this is how
you capture the hope
of the holiday season

70

You connect in a moment of quiet.
He seems happier when it's just him—
could be the noise level,
could be the attention,
who knows.
You have things to do,
but this doesn't happen much anymore;
you're not even sure
you know much about him
at this point.

He bought himself
a burger with money
he made from his first job.
You figure it won't take him
long to inhale it.
You'll stick around until he does.

He doesn't say a word
about video games or mods,
his normal subject matter.
You talk about
        the world,
        feminism,
        what problems you would change today

      to make a more equitable society.

These are the days
you get a glimpse of
who he might possibly be,
and you think,
Maybe I haven't ruined him.
Maybe he'll be the best of us.

This is how
you remember the kids
will be okay.

71

Today you let them
take care of breakfast.

One cooks the eggs,
another slices the English muffins,
then assembles the sandwiches.
One sets the table,
another hands out of the food.
It's a relief and a sorrow
to watch them at work,
see the very real evidence
of their growing up.

You let them do their thing,
and before long they've cleaned their plates,
darted outside,
stomped back in to tell you
about some indignity that
happened outside—
can you please step in
and help them right the wrong?

You know there's still
plenty more they need from you, even if
none of it will last forever.

It's probably better that
none of it will last forever.

For now, you give thanks
even for the arguments
that need you to resolve them.

This is how
you embrace the growing pains.

72

You sit around a long table
playing the most immature game

You laugh until you cry
everyone else joining you

It was the perfect game to bring—
this memory will go down
as a family favorite

And you'll say
This was a good day

This is how
you spend a late Christmas
with family

73

He says, *Don't forget*
you said you'd color
with me today!

Oh, yeah. You try not to groan.
You like coloring.
It's just…well,
of course there's so much to do.
You don't get much done
during the week,
because it's holiday break and
you're trying to enjoy
your time with them,
and now that it's the weekend
there's granola to bake,
organization to do,
pineapple to chop.

But you don't think about that.
You say, *Okay. Why not right now?*

He grins at you,
runs to get his coloring book.

This is how

you make a
seven-year-old's day.

74

You run fifteen miles
and a sixteenth to the end,
to cultivate the gratitude habit
you want to embrace
in the new year.

You finish a book.

You play board games
with your sons,
laugh until you cry,
share the joy of collaboration.

You text your mom and friends,
your husband who's sitting
across the room.

You discuss hopes, dreams,
plans for the year to come.

You eat, drink,
take them for a walk
and watch the magnificent sunset.

You end your day

with a shared show,
moved, peaceful, content.

This is how
you find hope in a brand-new year.

75

For so long you've felt
- flattened
- uninspired
- muted
- sad
- worried
- afraid
- tired
- unproductive
- stagnant
- ill-equipped
- frustrated
- overlooked
- uncreative
- lost
- cramped
- unappreciated
- forgotten
- distracted
- slow
- heavy
- beaten down
- lonely
- silenced
- disregarded

          ignored

uncertain

        wavering

weak

           timid

       undeserving

misunderstood

       desperate

breathless

           cemented

But today you join
an online conference
where you hear
you're not alone.

Today you think,
*Maybe I just need to give myself
permission to write
what I can write,
no matter what it looks like.*

Today you grab hold
of that dream,
shake it by the shoulders,
and say, *Someday you'll be mine
and I won't quit*

until you are.

This is how
you repair your wings.

76

It's an early-morning run,
hours before the sun's set to rise.

Your feet find their rhythm,
pacing out the miles,
carrying you over hills and depressions,
across fields and driveways,
through parking lots
practically empty so early.
You watch the landscape for
> animals,
> threats,
> any surprises that might lie in wait,

but a person can't plan for every surprise,
and when you lope past a swimming pool,
the sight makes you slow:
steam, rising in waves,
lifting into darkness,
a hazy blanket that hovers before vanishing,
like a breath blown from water,
dissolving into thin air.
The beauty of it almost lures you
into that pool—until you remember:
Not only do you have a run to finish,
but it's also forty degrees.

You turn back toward home,
your feet flying anew.

This is how
you fall in love (again)
with early morning runs.

77

Today you sit on an exam table
with a papery sheet draped
over your legs, your entire
backside exposed.
You never know quite what to do
with that papery sheet.
You wish the movies would show you,
since no one ever told you.
You feel a little self-conscious,
sitting here in this
bright-white room,
waiting.

Then the doctor breezes in,
finishes the exam in
less than five minutes,

and you think,
Did I really shave my legs
for this?

Oh, well.

This is how
you end a day with

silky smooth legs.

78

In the early morning hours,
you sneak down the stairs,
responsibilities mounting your shoulders already.
You didn't sleep well last night,
haven't slept well the last several nights,
and the last thing you really
want to do right now is
think about what's for breakfast.

And there,
      waiting in the place
      you usually sit,
is a bouquet of red roses,
a box of truffles,
and a note that confirms
you aren't actually invisible.

This is how
you begin a day remembering
you're loved and
seen and
appreciated.

79

Today you let him pull out
those sheets of stickers,
peel off dozens of red hearts,
pretend you don't see him
sticking them on
> light switches,
> your chair,
> your favorite mugs,

because he said,
Every time you see one of these,
it's me saying I love you,
and sometimes you need
to be reminded that
you're not a complete failure
at this thing called
motherhood.

You go hunting for hearts,
feel a jolt of joy every time
you find one.

This is how
you let yourself be loved.

80

In a moment of rare quiet,
while the voices of your children
lift and tilt in an unstoppable giggle outside,
you take out your pen and write,
the fragrance of dinner
swelling around you.

In another second
it will be over,
but for now…

This is how
you seize a moment.

81

Will you color with me? he says.

And today you have so much to do
today you are already behind
today a headache presses behind your eyes
urges you to get started
and fill in the gap as best you can

but today you
stretch out on the floor
gel pens beside you

and color with him.

This is how
you let yourself play.

82

You don't feel like working.

You had a hard time sleeping last night.
You're tired.
You feel very un-creative.
You have a lot on your mind.
You have things to do around the house.
You need more sleep.
You're probably burned out.
You've been dealing with
a pandemic for two years
plus inflation
plus the highs and lows of
        being a writer
plus teenage attitudes
plus kids on screens
plus strained family relationships
plus the world…

There are a hundred excuses
        probably more
and they're all valid.

You remind yourself
your work has a purpose.

You remind yourself
someone needs your words.
You remind yourself
there are no words if
you don't get to work.

You pick up your pen.
You write.

This is how
you talk yourself into carrying on.

83

Today you walk around the zoo,
watching your children watch animals

You've seen them all before
but what you really wanted to see today

the reason you took your seat
in a crowded van and walked for hours

even though you knew you'd likely
end your day with exhaustion and a headache

is you wanted to watch them
watch, point, grin

Sometimes the joy of others
can become your own and…you're trying

You really are
Nobody can say you aren't

This is how
you try to enjoy a day doused with depression

84

You walk through the house,
following them around with a camera.
You snap a picture of
> two reading together,
> two playing a board game together,
> a group of them making carvings from rock,
> a picture he hands you with the grin
>> that says he's proud.

And even though it's
an unexpected day off from school,
it is marvelous.

This is how
you bask in love.

free

85

you open the journal
write write pause
think
write write smile

the words flow
and before you know it
a whole day is gone
kids trip through the door
time speeds toward dinner

you think about it all the time
can't wait to take it in hand again
protect its time like a precious treasure
like one of your kids or your husband
like something beloved

you feel alive
exactly where you need to be
creating something beautiful
from the fragments of
      pain
      disappointment
      tribulation

where there was nothing
you offer something

the burn of passion
doesn't fade
with the light

you know you'll never really
work a day in your life
pursuing this passion

This is how
you find your purpose

86

Today you must talk to them about
>guns,
>school intruders,
>death.

You would rather talk to them about
anything else.

Today you walk them to school
and hope it's not the last time
you see them.

Today you hug them tight
and kiss them twice,
in case it is the last time
you see them.

Today you pray and hope
and pray that they
will return safely to you.

This is how
you make it through the day
after another school shooting.

87

Today you
        watch movies
        dance
        walk
        eat
        laugh
try your best to give every moment
your full attention
and even though
        by the end of it
you're more exhausted than
you've been in a long while

you tell yourself
you've done your best.

This is how
you make the most of a
Family Fun Day.

88

You finish your run
with a few minutes to spare.
They're at the pool.
You don't often join them
at the pool.
Call it insecurity,
call it body dysmorphia,
call it the thousands of other things
it may be.

They're ecstatic when you show up,
all of them trying to show you
some trick they learned between
the last time you came and now,
which you realize has been too long—
much too long.
They splash and laugh and play,
and you're glad you came.

You're glad you came.

Even stepping out of the water,
swimsuit sucking your curves,
your imperfect body on display,
              you're glad you came.

*When will you come with us
again?* they ask.
They always want to know,
want to make sure this
isn't the last time.

Soon, you say,
but inside you know:
Tomorrow.

This is how
you face your demons.

89

Today you let him climb on your lap
and wriggle into a comfortable position,
even though he's almost
too big to fit anymore.
You all watch a documentary.
You learn about communities
growing their own food,
potato preservation,
Blue Zones.
You hear them talking to each other
about starting a backyard garden,
choosing low-protein diets,
making decisions that benefit
their bodies and the environment.

You smile.
They're learning.
You're glad.

They say, *Can we watch one more?*
You're pretty sure it has more to do
with learning than with
the luxury of watching something.

You watch one more.

This is how
you grow together.

90

You watch him
walk into the restaurant
that employs him.
You've just had a
fifteen-minute conversation
about driver's ed and
the freedom that
a license can grant you.
He says he's not sure
he wants to learn to drive in America—
he's planning to move to Ireland
as soon as he graduates.
You think it's probably wishful thinking.
Or maybe you hope.

He sidesteps a puddle
on his way in the door.
He doesn't look back.
You send your love into the stratosphere
and hope he can feel it
every hour of his shift.

And when he texts,
Who's coming to get me? I get off at 3,
you're the smallest bit glad that

you've become his transportation
to and from work.
Whatever else happens,
at least you get fifteen uninterrupted minutes
to talk to him.

You don't waste a single one of them.
You're there when he opens his first paycheck
and when he learns how to deposit it.
You're there when he spends
the fruit if his first two working hours
on a footlong coney,
a mango cream slush,
and tater tots from Sonic.
You're there when he says,
I should have saved more of my money.
I'm kind of mad at myself
for spending it.

You think, *He's really growing up.*
You think, *Where did the time go?*
You think, *He's a good kid.*
He's going to be okay.

You think, *I'm so glad*
I get to be a part of his life.

This is how
you begin to let go.

91

You listen to her say
Your family is so remarkable
and you pause a moment
and let the words sink in
because sometimes in
the day-to-day grind
          you forget

You forget
how remarkable your family is
how remarkable your kids are
how remarkable *you* are

and

this is how
you remember

92

I might be wiggly tonight, he says.

That's okay, you say,
brushing the hair out of his eyes.
He blinks in the heavy way
that says he's tired.
It's been a while since
he fell asleep in your bed.
You want to memorize
>   the curve of his nose,
>   the curl of his eyelashes,
>   the way he seems to smile in his sleep.

He doesn't wiggle.
It doesn't even take him long
to fall asleep. He doesn't
let go of your hand.
You don't let go of his
until sleep sends both of you
in different directions and
his father returns him to his bed.

You dream of missing luggage.
It makes sense.
You're missing

their younger selves.
But you also adore
their present selves.

Such is the way of time.
You do what you can
to use it wisely and well.

This is how
you learn to let them fly.

93

They want you to play
a virtual reality game.
You want to read.
You could use the time
to hang out with them.
Or you could use it
to be by yourself.

It feels like an existential crisis:
                time to yourself
                or time with them?
You know you probably
won't win, either way.
Choose one, and you'll regret
not choosing the other.
It's why you hate making decisions.
You second guess yourself
on everything.

You go upstairs to read.
You block out the voice that says,
       They're growing up, you know.
       They won't be around forever.

You're growing up, too.

You won't be around forever.

You don't give it
another thought.

This is how
you take time to care for yourself.

94

Today was weigh-in day.
You've been working harder,
counting calories,
sweating through workouts—
sometimes too many in a day.
Your expectations are high,
but when you step on the scale,
it's not as low as it should be
according to your calculations.
You assess your past actions—
what went wrong?

You examine your body
in the mirror: What needs to change?
The answer to that question
would require a list much too long
for your taste.

The perfect body—
you'll settle for close to perfect now—
has been your quest all your life.

What do you do without it?

You're beautiful, he says,

pulling you into his arms.
You let him.
You don't have to try so hard
to be something you're not.
Who's perfect, anyway?

You let yourself believe him for today,
for this moment right here.

You let yourself be
enough.

This is how
you wrestle an eating disorder.

95

Today you walk three children
to school down the road,
ride in the front seat
beside your husband
to drop off two more
at the middle school,
send the last one to high school,
unbelievable as it is.

Today you have space again
to think, dream,
write write write.

This is how
you reset a summer
of stress.

96

You walk through
the amusement park you
used to visit all the time
when you were first married.
You can't ride as many rides anymore;
the twists and turns and
upside-down spins get your brain
agitated in a head-achy way.
But you hold hands and
sit beside each other and
laugh and groan at the stomach sickness
and bear the heat and
have a small tiny glimpse
of all those years ago,
when kids were hardly even
a consideration.
You remember what it's like
to be turned upside down and inside out
and walk off the ride still standing.

He takes your hand on the way out.
You practically skip to the car.
The years pass and pause.

You feel grateful

for every one.

This is how
you nurture a marriage.

97

Today you run a mile
but feel a niggling pain
in your hamstring.
A year ago, you would have
pushed through the pain,
and you would have regretted it,
because it would have ended
in a much longer injury.
But you're different now.
You give yourself breaks.
You know when enough
is enough—sometimes.

So you head back home
and finish a low-impact alternative.

You'd like to think you're getting better.
And maybe you are. Because

this is how
you know you're learning to
listen to your body.

98

One can't find his jacket
Another can't find his mask
The third's complaining about
not having any socks clean

You try not to rush
but you're six minutes off schedule
there's still a meandering walk to school
a brisk walk back
don't they know six minutes off schedule
makes the whole structure crumble?

They don't, of course
So you breathe in calm
breathe out peace
we'll just take a faster pace to school
they don't complain
they think it's fun
speed walking with their mom

This is how
you turn late into play

99

You take a walk

You do this every afternoon—
to clear your head,
to get your creativity flowing,
to mark the closing down of the day

Today is different

Today you walk through
a continuous cloud of butterflies
It's a magical experience,
like you're in some kind of fantasy world
They flutter around you,
carried by the wind but
beating their tiny wings in concert
You look up into the wild blue sky and smile—
you're so glad you're alive to see this,
to take a walk in a butterfly wonderland

*Who gets to experience
wonder like this?* you think
How many times have I missed it? you think
What can I do differently tomorrow? you think

A butterfly wing tickles your cheek

This is how
you hope

100

Today you watch
one of them read a book,
another stack cards,
two more tear through the backyard
on their way to secret places.

Today you melt
in your husband's smile,
stroke the gray along his temple,
talk about dreams and plans
and who's on pickup duty this week.

Today you feel alive,
moments burning through your brain,
searing themselves on memory cards,
speaking a truth you've
always known, probably:
Not every day will be like this.
Some days will be
>hard
>>unmanageable
>>>sad
>>filled with anxiety
>frustrating
>>a giant waste of time

                    unproductive
                disappointing
          terrible, horrible, no-good very bad days.

But some will be like today.

Some days you will fail.
Some days you will win.
Some you will wish away,
some you will wish could last

              forever.

Life equals all those days,
added up together,

                    the good
                    the bad
                    the ugly
                    the beautiful
                    the lowest drop of a valley
                    the highest lip of a mountain

You never know
what you'll get.
But you take them all,
and you live them
the best way you can.

This is how
you fly.

the end

About the Author

Rachel Toalson is the award-winning author of nine poetry books, including *this is how you know*, *Life: a definition of terms*, *The Book of Uncommon Hours*, *Textbook of an Ordinary Life*, *this is how you live*, *Sincerely Yours*, *Textbook of a Parenthetical Life*, and *Textbook of an Extraordinary Life*; three middle grade books; and multiple essay collections as well as books for children under a pen name. She has been writing poetry since the time she could hold a pencil and form what passed for letters on the page. Her first introduction to poetry was the brilliance of Shel Silverstein, whom she still reads with great pleasure today.

Her poems for children and adults can be read in literary magazines and online publications around the world.

Rachel lives with her husband and six children in San Antonio, Texas.

Author's Note

My dear reader,

What a strange time. If you are anything like me, you never, in your wildest imagination, thought you would live through a global pandemic. We all found ourselves in a weird world with all kinds of new and unexpected challenges and experiences. My house was never quiet, from March until November 2020, when we finally elected to send our kids back to school, because the virtual learning just wasn't working (and several of my normally brilliant sons were failing classes). It took even longer to quiet my mind.

We are still recovering.

Mental health and wellbeing took a hit during COVID. We found ourselves isolated and unable to connect with friends and even family members. Some of us found ways around it, like setting up chairs six feet apart in our driveways just to have a little company. Here in Texas, we experienced a snowstorm that knocked out our power for days. We had to share resources while COVID was still going strong in 2021. We found new ways of living and being. I'm a homebody, but I could not wait to get back out into the world, to sit in a restaurant and watch people, to go walk downtown and not feel like I was entering a ghost town.

But make no mistake—we are still recovering. Any time we find ourselves disconnected from community, isolated in ways we were not meant to live, we'll have some recovery ahead of us.

It's my hope that this book will help. That it will not only help those still climbing out of their isolation and stretching into their new normal to feel less alone in their experiences and emotions but it will also shine a light on the most difficult places that still take up space in our minds and hearts. Things always seem completely unmanageable and never-ending when we're in the middle of them. But looking back, we can make some sense of them. We can begin to see the silver lining. That's what writing this book did for me—and what I hope it does for you.

In the darkest of times it helps to remember we're not alone. Take heart. You're stronger than you know. And we're stronger together. Keep moving forward. Unfold your wings and fly.

I'll see you in the skies.

In love,
Rachel

P.S. Please don't forget to leave a review and share this book with your friends. Reviews help other readers know whether this is a book they'd like to have on their shelves, and when we share books with friends, we are giving authors one of the greatest gifts we can give: a word-of-mouth recommendation. A writer is indebted to those who pass along their book with a genuine "You should read this." Thank you!

Acknowledgments

Nothing in life is a solitary effort—even a global pandemic, when you're sheltering in place. I'm grateful to so many people for helping me have the strength and fortitude to endure such a challenging time—which led to the strength and fortitude to write this book of poetry.

Ben: Well, we had some good times and bad times, but I cannot imagine a better partner than you by my side. I'm also grateful that you survived it all with me and that you didn't even blink when I said, "I think I have a new poetry book. It's about the pandemic."

Jay, Asa, Hosea, Boaz, Zadok, and Asher: While the pandemic was a challenging, restless time, you endured it with patience and love, and I am so grateful for the time we had together—however wild and out of control it might have been.

Quarantine Club: Our time out in driveways, with six feet of space between us, was a lifesaver. Having adult conversations and the space to discuss how hard it was to spend all day with kids, making sure they did their virtual learning, what it was like to crumble under cabin fever…I don't know how we would have survived without the camaraderie of friends going through the same thing.

Community matters.

All my kids' teachers: Thanks for doing the best you could—and being patient with all your students.

Poets who kept me company during the worst of days: Thank you for your words.

The poetry community: Thank you for keeping me on track and inspiring me to write.

And the Zoombies: You will be thanked forever after, for your friendship, wise words, and support. It's amazing how brave solidarity makes you. Thank you for commiserating, challenging, and always encouraging. What a phenomenal group of writers, friends, and human beings.

Enjoy more titles from Rachel Toalson

racheltoalson.com

Rachel Toalson Poetry
Starter Library

Enjoy more of Rachel Toalson's poetry with these free downloads.

To get your FREE books, visit *
RachelToalson.com/FreeBook

*Must be 13 or older to be eligible

www.ingramcontent.com/pod-product-compliance
Lightning Source LLC
Chambersburg PA
CBHW030443090526
44586CB00044B/587